# Faith Nuggets
## *To Live By*

## Dr. Jawanza Kunjufu

**African American Images**
**Chicago, IL**

Front cover illustration by Angelo Williams

Copyright © 2012 by Dr. Jawanza Kunjufu

All rights reserved.

First Edition, First Printing

Printed in the United States of America

ISBN #: 1-934155-65-9
ISBN #: 978-1-934155-65-3

# Contents

Introduction                                    v

1. What is faith?                               1

2. What size is your faith?                     7

3. How essential is faith?                      19

4. How does faith come?                         23

5. How does faith work?                         27

6. When is faith present?                       35

7. Faith Nuggets                                47

A Man of Faith                                  119

# Introduction

After salvation, faith is the most important subject in the Bible. **Hebrews 11:6** *(NKJV)* reminds us, "without faith it is impossible to please Him." This book is filled with faith nuggets. We often read the Bible and expect it to have hundreds of pages on marriage, health, parenting and other topics. Sometimes the Bible may only have three verses on a particular topic. It is imperative that we begin to meditate *on* the Word of God *and* not just read

for information but for revelation. This book is
filled with faith nuggets based on the Word of God,
not to be read for information, but to be *meditated*
on and gleaned for *revelation*.

# Chapter 1: What is faith?

Faith is the substance of things hoped for, the evidence of things unseen. If faith is the evidence, then faith is real. In **Hebrews 11,** the words faith, hope, and believe often are used interchangeably. They are in the same family of meaning, but they are not the same. Note the difference between faith and hope in **Hebrews 11:1**. Hope is the object or desire, but faith is the title deed, the evidence, the assurance, the foundation you use that you will secure what you have hoped for. Faith is a noun and believe is a verb. Hope says I will get it in the future. Faith says I have it **now**. The simplest definition of faith is acting like the Bible is true. Kenneth Hagin, Sr. said that before praying for a person's healing, he would ask them if they "will" be healed when he would lay hands on them. If they said they "hope" they will be healed, Hagin told them they won't because they are in hope not faith. Hope is future tense and faith is current tense.

The same applies to believe and faith. To believe is to desire, to hope for, it requires no foundation or work. Faith is the corresponding action to your belief. More will be offered about these words throughout the book. Fred Price says, "The greatest enemy to faith is ignorance of the Word of God."

Your faith must understand the stages of harvest. First the blade (the seedling or young plant), then the ear (the blossoming), followed by the fully ripened manifestation. Your faith must be patient and confident.

In **Genesis 32:24-28,** Jacob wrestled with God and would not let Him go until He blessed him. You must develop bulldog faith. In **Mark 5:35,** they told Jairus, "Your daughter is dead." Jesus said to Jairus and now to you, "Do not be afraid; only believe" (**Mark 5:36**). Jesus then healed his daughter, like He will for you.

Faith is not a feeling, it's a choice, it's a decision. You must bind every thought and image that contradicts your faith and the Word of God.

# Chapter 2: What size is your faith?

*Oh you of little faith*
Matthew 6:30

*Faith the size of a mustard seed*
Matthew 17:20

*Full of faith*

Acts 6:5

*Sufficient faith*

I Corinthians 13:2

*Growing faith*
II Corinthians 10:15

*Rich in faith*
James 2:5

*Genuine faith*

I Peter 1:7

*Firm faith*
      I Peter 5:9

*Holy faith*

Jude 1:20

*Great faith*
   Matthew 8:10

*Strong faith*

Romans 4:20

*Righteousness of faith*
Phillippians 3:9

# Chapter 3: How essential is faith?

It's as important as air and water. Your salvation and gift of eternal life is based on faith. **Romans 10:9** *(NKJV)* says, "If you confess with your mouth the Lord Jesus and believe in your heart that God raised Him from the dead, you will be saved." "The just shall live by faith" (**Hebrews 10:38**). Living by faith is not something you do just when you're hoping or believing. Living by faith is not reserved for a crisis. Andrew Wommack said, "God gives you grace and our part is to receive it by faith." Every time you receive the physical manifestation of what you were believing God for, it builds your confidence and you are moving from faith to faith. You must have faith in your faith. You must be able to tell your story of what God has done for you. You cannot ride the faith of your grandparents, parents, pastor, spouse, siblings, or anyone else. You must develop and use your faith. For the rest of your life, you must live by faith. Faith for the promise is in the promise (God's word). Faith says the same thing the Bible says. Many unbelievers say, "if it be Thy will for me to be healed". The word *if* illustrates their doubt and to use *Thy will,* which is God's Word indicates they are not aware that God has already healed us by His stripes. The greatest enemy to faith is doubt.

The Bible reminds us in **II Corinthians 5:7**, *(KJV)* "For we walk by faith not by sight." You don't walk or talk by how you feel. You must walk by faith. For the rest of your life you must walk by faith not by sight. You can no longer place your five senses before your faith. Sight or the five senses is the opposite of faith. Faith is the sixth sense, or actually, I would prefer to call faith the first sense followed by the other five. A pilot learns to fly by relying on the instruments because often they cannot see much of anything. To walk by faith you must believe the Word of God. Do not look at things because they are subject to change. Things are not the proof. Faith is the proof. **Ephesians 2:8** reminds us that you are saved through your faith. Jesus is the author and finisher of your faith (see **Hebrews 12:2**). Your faith can make you well. Just ask blind Bartimaeus, described in **Mark 10:52** or the bleeding woman in **Matthew 9:20-22**. The only fight the believer is called upon to fight, is the good fight of faith. It's a good fight because you always win. You cannot lose a fight of faith— you can only quit a fight of faith. If you've got joy in the middle of a fight, then you are walking by faith.

There is a difference between head knowledge and heart faith (**see I Timothy 6:11-16**). Satan wants you to believe with your mind, flesh, and five senses. He wants you to believe in the natural. God wants you to believe with your heart (**see Romans 10:10**).

# Chapter 4: How does faith come?

Faith comes by hearing, and hearing the Word of God (see **Romans 10:17**). When you got saved, your spirit got saved, not your soul or flesh. You will spend the rest of your life in a war between your spirit, who wants you to live for God and your flesh (a mind-set), who wants you to live for the pleasure of his five senses. Your soul is the determining factor. God gave you the truth and Satan gave you a lie. You are the deciding witness. The decision will be based on whether your soul will receive more word from God or from the world. Your faith will come by hearing the word of God. Faith does not come by praying. It is a gift from God that only comes by hearing and believing His word.

Faith is like a muscle. Everyone is born with the same level of faith. God does not give one person more faith than another person has. God does not show favoritism (see **Acts 10:34**). God has dealt to each one a measure of faith (see **Romans 12:3**). You must develop your faith. The greatest hindrances to your faith are fear and doubt. More people die of the fear of cancer than the actual cancer. Their fear is greater than their faith. Fear is faith in the devil. They both come from Satan. God gave you the authority to bind both of them. Developing your faith is like making a cake. You have to mix God's Word with your faith. Fred Price says, "The mixing bowl is your mouth and the beater blade is your tongue."

Faith comes by hearing the Word of God. Your faith needs a foundation. What Scriptures are you basing your faith on? You cannot develop your faith with one sermon. You must continue to hear the Word of God. Could they not hear the voice behind the verse? Bishop David Oyedepo says, "The voice of God is the stronghold of faith." Satan can only destroy you through your mind. Satan does not want you to have faith in God and His Word.

# Chapter 5: How does faith work?

Jesus said to the two blind men, "Do you believe that I am able to do this?" They said to Him, "Yes, Lord." Then He touched their eyes, saying, "According to your faith let it be to you." And their eyes were opened. (**Matthew 9:27-30,** paraphrased). **Notice the Scripture did not say His faith; it's *your* faith. It also did not say according to your income, education, race, gender, family background, or anything else but your faith.**

You start with your belief. You start with something hoped for. You then bring it into fruition with your faith. Let's review the above Scripture. Jesus wants you to believe He can achieve what you have hoped for. It is not the size of your faith, but the size of the God you believe in that will determine the size of your harvest. Your faith grows with your love for God. Do you have faith in the name of Jesus? This is different than you believing you can do it. In the secular world people have high expectations of themselves. There is a difference between faith in God and the power of positive thinking or science of the mind. Oral Roberts once said, "The important thing is not the size of your faith, it is the One behind your faith—God Himself." **Hebrews 12:2** *(NKJV)* says,

"Looking unto Jesus, the author and finisher of our faith." Notice God wants you to believe He can do it but it's according to your faith. Not His faith. Not your ability, degree, race, income, good looks, etc. That's why this subject is so important because everything you need, desire, or want will come according to your faith. Even Jesus could only perform a few miracles in His hometown because of their little faith. Can you imagine you can block the power of God according to your faith? In **Mark 9:23** *(NKJV)* we read, "If you can believe, all things are possible to him [and her] who believes." What are you believing God for? If what you are believing God for can be achieved by you, then it's too small for God. How big is your God? Is there anything too large or impossible for God? In **Genesis 13:15** *(NLT)*, God told Abraham, "I am giving all this land, as far as you can see, to you and your descendants." How far can you see? Your faith is contingent upon how far you can see.

**James 2:20** *(KJV)* says, "Faith without works is dead." Until you do it you have not believed the Word.

Many people have beliefs and hopes but no faith. This is illustrated by their lack of works, their corresponding inaction. In **Luke 17:11-19,** Jesus told the 10 lepers to show themselves to the priest and they would be healed. When were they healed? When the priest saw them? No. They were healed when they took their first step toward the priest. Their first step was an illustration of their faith. It was their corresponding action. Faith can be seen. You sow and reap in faith. Blind Bartimaeus in **Mark 10:50** threw away his beggar's clothes because he had the faith to know Jesus was going to heal him of his blindness and he would no longer have to beg. When was he healed? When he threw away his clothes. God wants to see your faith.

Everything in the Kingdom of God operates by faith. It is the answer to every question. God needs to see your faith. The more Word of God you hear and believe, the greater your faith. How many hours of God's Word do you hear daily? How much secular news do you hear daily? No word—no faith; little word—little faith; much word—much faith.

If your faith is not at the level of your hope you must strengthen your faith. **Galations 3:14** *(NKJV)* says, "that the blessing of Abraham might come upon the Gentiles in Christ Jesus, that we might receive the promise of the Spirit through faith." Your blessing from God is dependent on your level of faith. The greatest illustration of your faith can be found in your praise. Faith sees the end result. Faith always has a good report.

Seed faith is giving something you have for something you desire. God is not moved by your need or your tears. He is moved by your faith and your seed. Seed faith is giving something you have for something you desire. In Hebrews 4:2," Fore we also have the gospel preached to us, just as they did, but the message they heard was of no value to them, because those who heard did not combine it with faith." You can go to church every Sunday, hear thousands of sermons and read your Bible every day, but without faith you will not receive God's best.

In **Hebrews 11,** the faith hall of fame, the men and women listed in these verses lived and died in faith. They finished the race in faith. Do you have finishing faith? Stubborn faith? Radical faith? Sold out faith? Abraham is considered the father of faith; but remember, he was about 117 when he was going to sacrifice Isaac, a very strong 17-year-old. Isaac could have easily stopped Abraham. Do you have the faith of Isaac that your heavenly daddy will take care of you?

What you conceive, you believe. The God kind of faith is conceive, believe, speak, and see. To receive God's best you must believe He is a good God. You cannot believe those who tell you that when something bad happens to you God is trying to teach you something. You must believe **John 10:10** *(NASB)*, which speaks of Satan: "The thief comes only to steal and kill and destroy; I have come that they may have life, and have it abundantly." You must believe that.

# Chapter 6: When is faith present?

Faith is now, says **Hebrews 11:1.** Tradition and your carnal mind will always try to get you to believe that your blessing is in the future. Your healing, job, marriage, child, whatever you are believing God for is in the future. Blessed be the God and Father of our Lord Jesus Christ who has blessed us with every spiritual blessing (read **Ephesians 1:3).** By whose stripes were you healed? (Read **I Peter 2:24.**) **Faith is now, hope is future tense. I** *believe* **God is going to heal me is not faith.**

You already have your healing, job, marriage, children, whatever you are believing God for. You have it by faith. Your job is to show some corresponding action. My pastor, Bill Winston shares the following story: "If a prospective employer told you that you have the job on Friday, you would spend the rest of the weekend preparing for work on Monday. Why would you believe the employer more than God?" The weatherman says tomorrow will be hot and you believe and dress accordingly. God wants you to believe Him like you did the employer and weatherman. God has 7,874 promises for you in the Bible.

**Galations 5:6** *(KJV)* says, "but faith . . . worketh by love." You can read your Bible and pray every minute of your life, you can read your confession every day of your life, you can tithe and offer all your income, but if you are not walking in love, if you have not forgiven everybody your faith has no power. Unforgiveness is the thief of faith. Be quick to forgive, repent, and believe. Your faith and your victory are in jeopardy if you are living in sin. Strife steals your faith. Is there any strife in your house?

Faith is voice activated. **Proverbs 18:21** *(KJV)* reminds us, "Death and life are in the power of the tongue." **Romans 4:17** says that God calls things that do not exist as though they do exist. I want you to read carefully **Mark 11:23-24** *(KJV)*. Count the times it uses the word *say*. Count the times it uses the word *pray*. Three times it uses *say*. One time it says *pray*. **You do not get what you pray for, you get what you say.** Bishop Clarence McClendon connects it to law enforcement: "You have the right to remain silent, anything you say can and will be held against you." Pastor Winston describes it to being a pilot; you must say exactly what the air traffic controller said. Pastor Nasir Saddiki parallels it with **Hebrews 4:12** and the two-edged sword. This sword represents God saying it first and you repeating it back verbatim. There is no faith without confession. If you can't say what God said then be silent. Confession is faith's way of expressing itself.

Faith never rises above or below your confession. Your confession is the best barometer of your faith. Author Mark Hankins says, "Your voice is your address in the Spirit. Your voice is the highway your angels travel. If your faith is not talking, it is not working." Speaking is how you release your faith. Out of the abundance of the heart the mouth speaks. You cannot pray in church that you are healed and talk to your friends about "your" illness. The Shunamite woman (**II Kings 4:8-37**) in the natural knew her son was dead but to her husband and Elisha she held fast to her confession of faith (see **Hebrews 10:23**), and she said, "It is well!" Her faith healed her son.

You must hold fast to your confession of faith because Satan is trying to take away your faith. Many people get tired of holding fast and they lack patience. Paul wrote in **2 Corinthians 4:13** *(KJV)*, "I believed, and therefore have I spoken." When you speak your faith your corresponding action must back it up. You do not call things the way you "wish" but the way they are. The doctor says you are sick. That is a fact and subject to change. **Second Corinthians 4:18** *(NKJV)* says, "While we do not look at the things which are seen, but at the things which are not seen. For the things which are seen are temporary (your sickness, poverty, and poor relationships), but the things which are not seen (God's 7,874 promises) are eternal." The Bible says you are healed. That is the truth and will not change. You must ask yourself, whose report will you believe?

Faith grows in confession. Pastor Winston says, "Words filled with faith are more powerful than nuclear bombs." Confession is faith expressing itself. Confession brings possession. You will say what you believe. You pray your request once in faith. All subsequent prayers on that request are prayers of thanksgiving. If you continue to make the request, you insult God and assume He did not hear you and you illustrate you are in hope and not faith. The late Pastor Smith Wigglesworth said, "If you prayed seven times for the same concern then you prayed six times in unbelief." It's obvious that you keep praying because you did not see it in the natural. Thomas needed to see Jesus to believe (**John 20:24-28**), while Abraham believed God's Word (**Genesis 15:6**). What you see and how you feel have nothing to do with faith. As is written in **Mark 11:24,** it's important to meditate on four of the most important words in the Bible: **"I believe, I receive."**

One of the greatest challenges in the church is tithing. Less than 25% of Christians are tithers and some studies say it's 7%. God does not need our money. All of the earth belongs to Him. God knows how much we value money and how much time we spend earning and thinking about it. For some, we have made money our god. The Lord wants to find out if you have enough faith to give Him 10% and believe you will live a better life off 90% than those who have 100%. You say you love God, SHOW ME YOUR FAITH!

If you do not have enough faith in God to tithe, how do you have enough faith to believe you are going to heaven?

Fear is the opposite of faith. When you are in fear you do not believe God, you believe Satan. When you are in faith you believe God and His word. Faith is like a muscle that needs to be developed. Start developing your faith for small things. Don't start believing God to remove your cancer when you have not used your faith to remove a cold. Some people become super-spiritual; they decide not to use medication. They believe they are only healed by His stripes. God has more than a trillion ways to heal and one of those could be medication. Let the Holy Spirit guide you.

Some people confuse faith with fraud. They give the church a million dollar check with insufficient funds. Faith is the substance of things hoped for (giving the church a million dollar check) and the evidence (sufficient funds, the physical manifestation). Keep the faith check at home and only give the church the check with physical manifestation.

The size of your faith determines God's supply. Faith is developed in your praise. Your words reflect your faith. If what you are believing God for can be achieved by you, it's too small for God. Faith is the seed for your healing, deliverance, and prosperity. Faith is developed by meditating on God's Word.

Throughout the book, we have written that faith is now and hope is in the future. Compare **Isaiah 53:5,** *NKJV* ("And by His stripes we are healed") to **I Peter 2:24,** *NKJV* ("by whose stripes you were healed"). Is faith past or present? **Ephesians 1:3** *(NKJV)* reads, "Blessed be the God and Father of our Lord Jesus Christ, who has blessed us with every spiritual blessing." Is faith past or present? Nothing takes place on Earth until it has taken place spiritually. Whatever you believe God for (in the present) has already happened (in the past). Your healing took place over 2,000 years ago when Jesus paid for it on the Cross. Author E. W. Kenyon said, "The largest percentage of those who are healed in mass meetings, have mass faith and seldom maintain their healing. They have no personal faith. They had the faith of the people present at the mass meeting."

# Chapter 7: Faith Nuggets

It is not the size of your faith, but the ONE behind your faith.

Have faith in God. Have the God kind of faith.

Confession is faith's way of expressing itself.

The greatest enemy to faith is doubt. Faith that cannot be seen cannot manifest in the Earth.

How strong is your faith? Is it strong in all areas?

Do you have strong faith for your salvation? Your

finances? Your relationships? Your healing? How

long will you stay in faith? A week? A month? A

year? A decade? A lifetime?

Faith opens the door to God's promises and patience keeps it open. Read **Hebrews 6:12.**

Can you stay in faith under pressure? When you're broke? Unemployed? Sick? Experiencing family challenges?

Don't wait for a crisis to develop your faith.

Develop your faith *before* the crisis.

Faith for the promise (in the present) is in the promise (the past).

Your confession is in the present.

Unforgiveness will stunt your faith walk. Faith does not believe what the world says is impossible, because with God all things are possible. Some people believe God for nothing and that is exactly what they receive. Living by faith is a lifestyle, not something reserved for a crisis.

How strong is your faith? As long as it takes faith and it won't take long.

Believing is a choice, not a feeling.

Nothing happens on Earth until it is spoken.

Faith is acting on what you believe. Faith is released by your actions. What is the difference between the grace of faith in **Romans 12:3** and the gift of faith in **I Corinthians 12:9?** Is the former used for salvation and the latter for miracles?

Don't see the problem, visualize the promise. Have faith in the promise. The Word is the promise. Your faith must be seen. It must be released. Everything you desire from God is according to your faith.

Faith works, but you have to work it. Don't let your faith stagnate. Faith is the most important force in the world. How can faith be so powerful and so many people are impotent?

Faith is your access to God. Faith is the key to every door you want opened. Pastor Winston says, "Faith is the currency of the kingdom."

Faith is your confidence in God's Word. Faith works where the will (God's Word) is known. Faith that has not produced any fruit is fake.

It does not need to make sense if it makes faith. Faith cannot fail.

Faith is a spiritual weapon. Radical faith is deciding not to live like the crowd. Peter left the crowd on the boat and walked on the water (**Matthew 14:28-30**). The faith fight occurs in the mind. You cannot win the faith fight with an unrenewed mind.

You cannot have faith for something you have not

heard. You must believe God wants you to have good

health; a marriage made in heaven; saved,

obedient, and accomplished children; and wealth

and riches in your house.

Pastor Nasir Saddiki says, "God measures your faith by your seed."

Faith not tested is faith not proven. Fair weather faith is not faith. Faith requires a storm. Walking by faith requires courage and persistence.

Faith is a law and will work for anyone who understands it.

Is God pleased with your faith?

Faith always finds a way. Faith believes, confesses, works, praises, and rests. The size of your faith determines God's supply.

Faith is the answer to every question. Faith is the master key that will open any door. When you have the Word, you have the check.

No faith comes from your head. Satan wants to destroy your faith. Faith joins you to the anointing.

When you decide to walk by faith, you don't get rid of trials. Your faith overcomes them.

Faith is the master key.

You serve a God of no limits. Take the limits off your faith.

You must conquer your challenge by faith.

Do you believe your job or your God is your source?

Pastor Winston says, "You are where you are because of what you desire.

You are where you are based on your level of faith.

Continue in the faith.

Colossians 1:23

Faith comes by hearing not just from the Bible or from the preacher. Faith comes by hearing what you say.

Your confession will not work if you do not believe what you say.

Everything you are believing God for is paid by His Blood.

Create a picture of your desire to increase your faith.

Faith will take you and keep you where no one else can.

To walk by faith you cannot conform to this world's way of thinking.

Take the limits off your faith, because your God has no limits.

You don't become what you want, you become what you believe.

Faith is now and worry is always concerned about the future.

God permits your faith to determine your destiny.

Do not allow the logic of your mind to collide with the faith in your heart. James 1:5-7, "But let him ask in faith without doubting."

If you doubt you cut off God's gift of faith.

Without faith it is impossible to become one with God—Faith is total trust.

Faith is the substance (healing, salvation, marriage, job, house, car, whatever you are believing from God).

Does God believe in you more than you believe in Him?

The beauty of children is they believe what you tell them.

Do you believe what God told you in His Word?

If you can doubt, you can believe. They are both your decisions.

Either the circumstance will change your faith or your faith will change the circumstance.

Do you run your life, family, finances, health, eternity, everything by faith?

It does not have to make sense if it makes faith.

Your job is to believe God and speak His Word.

Faith is your confidence.

God is not a respecter of person, but is a respecter of your faith.

My wife says" you can have the faith for something, but not the patience." It requires both.

You must believe God that you have it now in the spirit and have the patience to wait until it appears in the physical.

Those who have strong faith wait in confidence.

You cannot fight a faith fight in the flesh.

Faith will not take no for an answer.

If you want more from God you must say more of His Word.

Live or die, you must stand in faith. Pastor Winston says "faith sees the invisible.

"Faith sees what God says. Leroy Thompson says"

I don't see what I don't lack. I see what I lack."

The devil believes that God exists. Charles Stanley calls that intellectual faith and many Christians possess it. Saving faith requires a heart relationship.

You are a triune being. Your spirit, soul and body must all walk by faith.

Faith is a spirit not a feeling.

Faith is your servant, make him work for you.

Everything you are believing God for is paid by His Blood.

Create a picture of your desire to increase your faith.

Faith will take you and keep you where no one else can.

To walk by faith you cannot conform to this world's way of thinking.

Take the limits off your faith, because your God has no limits.

You don't become what you want, you become what you believe.

Faith is now and worry is always concerned about the future.

Your eyes are made to see not believe.

Your ears are made to hear not believe.

Your brain is made to think not believe.

Only your heart was made to believe.

Are you willing to sacrifice all you have for what you believe?

What you focus on is what you magnify.

Faith demands it becomes your only source.

Only faith moves God.

Faith is a law (Romans 3:27).

What you believe determines the quality of your life.

Once you get in faith, your destiny cannot be denied.

When you have faith, you wait with great excitement.

Creflo Dollar says, "faith is not a movement, it's a prescription for living."

God will allow you to go as far as your faith will take you.

Faith is your evidence.

You cannot live a life of faith without His joy.

Faith will make your job.

Faith will pay your bills.

Faith will find your spouse.

Faith will heal you.

Faith will save your family members.

To walk by faith, you must keep your eye on God's word.

Your faith cannot help you avoid storms, but it will help you overcome them.

Hope comes before faith.

Joy and hope encourage you while you are waiting in faith.

Pastor Leroy Thompson says "Faith and hope are your dancing partners."

You must develop and perfect your faith.

(I Thessalonians 3:30).

You can't use $5 faith for a $5,000 problem.

If you don't have faith for removing a headache, then you don't have faith to remove cancer.

Start at the level of your faith.

Living by faith is not something you try. Its a lifestyle. You do it when it's easy or hard.

Only your faith will carry you through life.

Faith comes by hearing not just the Word of God but His voice behind His Word.

# A Man of Faith

Alexander Kerr was the founder of Kerr Glass

Manufacturing Company, which had a factory

in San Francisco. He became a believer and a

tither. He believed **Malachi 3:11** *(KJV)*,

"And I will rebuke the devourer for your sakes,

and he shall not destroy the fruits of your

ground." Kerr became very rich. There was

a massive earthquake in 1906 that created

terrible fires and the citizens had to evacuate.

He was told his business would be destroyed.

He responded by saying that if that were

true, God's Word was a lie. He stood on

**Malachi 3:11.** The entire block was destroyed

except his factory—even though it was the most

flammable structure, including the

surrounding wooden fence!

God's Word is true and will not come back void,

but will accomplish what it has been sent to

achieve (see **Isaiah 55:11**).

You are the righteousness of God. You are a

joint heir with Jesus. He calls you friend. He

died and rose just for you!

I pray you will continue to walk and live

by faith and receive all of God's promises

for your life.


*Shalom* (completeness, wholeness, nothing

missing)!

# Jawanza Kunjufu

## is Coming to Your Church:

Faith Sunday

Men's Sunday

Health Sunday

Youth Sunday

Family Sunday

Graduation Sunday

Black History Sunday

Father's Day

P.O. Box 1799  ♦  Chicago Heights, IL 60412  ♦  Phone 708/672-4909  ♦  Fax 708/672-0466
www.AfricanAmericanImages.com  ♦  e-mail address: customersvc@africanamericanimages.com